The Concept of Critters

Tryniti Thresher

BookLeaf Publishing

Presentation by *BookLeaf Publishing*

Web: www.bookleafpub.com

E-mail: info@bookleafpub.com

ISBN: 9789357440172

First edition 2023

I am dedicating this, my first chapbook, to the people who surround me and keep me on my toes (and out of my head).

To my partner in life, who is so damn easy to love and fall in love with again and again every day.

To my midnight family; Pointy, Dirty, Fiend, Shiro, and Tom.

To my best friend Amanda who has a sweet heart and wicked tongue.

To my little brother Jack, who loves quietly but just as fiercely as anyone I've ever known.

To a boundless spirit of a woman with poetry in her fingers and beauty in her smile; Casey, my half-sister.

And to everyone else who shaped and formed and molded me into the odd thing I am today; a person that never stops looking around and within herself to find meaning and connection. Even in something like a flatworm.

ACKNOWLEDGEMENT

There is no friend like a bosom buddy, a kindred spirit, a soul sister that just 'gets' you, and spurs you on to be your best self while (metaphorically or otherwise) holding your hair back during times of weakness. For me, that is my best and closest friend of nearly two decades, Amanda Hawk. She is a master poet who has been writing herself for years. Her support and encouragement during some of my darkest days keep me going, and I do not take for granted the steel she wields in cutting down my pieces which need reshaping and an unrelenting eye.

Amanda is also the reason I began taking poetry classes, exposing me to wondrous worlds within literature and therein finding the techniques I needed to elevate my own work.

That is also how I was introduced to Megan Falley, an incredibly dedicated and articulate mentor who is well-known in the poetry scene for her witty and charming pieces about love and childhood.

With her 'Poetry That Doesn't Suck Class' inspiring poets around the world and helping them through the creative writing and editing process, she taught me that I cannot be held hostage to the whims of striking inspiration, but rather should harness and reign over my own creative process.

These two amazing (and I feel that word is overused but, in this case, it's very appropriate) women inspire me and I cannot thank them enough simply for being who they are.

My husband Jeremiah is also deserving of all the praise I can give him. His ability to make me laugh when I'm feeling down, build me up when I need to know I am not broken, and unfalteringly encourage me down whatever path leads toward the dreams I hold that day is invaluable and rare.

He is the kindest, most intelligent, and most thoughtful man I have ever known. Thank you, darling, for offering me your hand and your heart. I'll keep them safely in mine, walk the path toward our dreams together, and always choose you as my Pokemon.

PREFACE

"In all things of nature, there is something of the marvelous." - Aristotle

As a nerd and a poet, I am enchanted with the presentation of learning through beautiful words.

My hope for you is that the poems within this book will inspire an enthusiastic journey of discovery. That you will learn not only about the world we live in but about yourself.

It's exciting to learn something new. And it is changes of mind that make us grow. It's the chance you're willing to take to do so that sets you apart. What creature will you open your heart to? What odd being will you end up identifying with the most?

Enjoy the journey, and know that ultimately, you are a singular organism on this crazy place we call Earth, and in this way alone you are connected to all the rest.

The Transparent Tadpole

Dripping from leaves
into soft water below
a delicate life
drifts away in the flow.

They are bare to the world
showing everything inside
vulnerable and unclouded,
they've nothing to hide.

Clear as glass
they find their own way
tiny and elusive,
with hearts on display.

Blanch the Nudibranch

I am soft and small,
but a wee stormy thing,

storing tactical toxins
for a poisonous sting.

Beautiful to some,
and unsightly to others,

I am a mystery
of many different colors.

I may be strange,
and hard to accept -

in the shallows
of the tropics,
is where I am kept.

Please handle with care;
for those unaware -
I cannot breathe
in simple air.

I inhale through my skin

to the haemolymph within,

and I must admit,
I do it with flair.

The Hawaiian Bobtail Squid
and Aliivibrio Fischeri

Tiny speck in a universe-sized ocean
in harmony unites with other tiny specks.

And together do they set into motion
an effect as beautiful as it is complex.

Quorum sensing to seek their density
gives rise to a tiny miraculous show,

made no less exquisite by its mild intensity,
of setting a symbiotic body aglow.

Mild Moon Jelly

A transparent tranquility floats
on unforgiving currents.
A delicate-looking entity of note
resists the sea's wildest deterrents.
Battered by the waves
a baby moon survives
untamed and unwittingly brave
not to be judged for its size.

For while the modest sting
of this translucent being
is a rare and fruitless thing.
Its will, you see,
to survive is immense
and sometimes that can be
the only required defense.

Plight of the Pleco

A prehistoric catfish glides in her armor
through lakes and streams,
where she may live out her days
in the home of her dreams.

For she grows quite large,
an adult two feet long -
making the common aquarist's tank
sizing all wrong.

Her true lifespan is meant
to take up twenty years,
but smaller and younger
than her disappear.

This pretty plated pleco
is a common victim of myth;
"Only growing to the size of their aquarium",
a saying that plagues many fish.

Development stunted
in a space too small,
life in a home that won't fit you
is no life at all.

She's been around a long time
and is more than scale and bone
she is a 'bottom-feeder',
with a beauty all her own.

Spotted Dotted Wobbegong

I am a fleshy-tasseled bearded mouth
dotted with spots for nocturnal plots.
A carpet-level predator
caved at daybreak
near rock reefs and colored coral
castles of an Indian Ocean make.

Flattened head and body
to smooth against the stream,
spiracles silently soaking
up the oxygen of the sea
so while motionless
I may breathe.

These vestigial temples rest
behind almond-shaped eyes,
low-light adapted
for nighttime goodbyes.

Fire God of Xochimilco

A teacup-sized amphibian
rumored Aztec god of old,
disguised himself as a salamander
turning his hot blood cold.

This marvel on four legs stole
from a neotenic fountain of youth
to keep his adolescent form
and forever hide the truth.

Dubbed the Mexican walking fish
he has an axe to grind
with the likes of newts and olms
his more sophisticated kind.

With La Gioconda modesty he smiles
in the Mexico Valley lake
engulfing worms and insects
in a body he can't escape.

But some divine power lingers
regenerating organs and limbs,
dreaming of the day he returns
from the shallows where he swims.

The Reasonable Radiolaria

Predatory beings live
in unicellular form -
neither animal nor plant,
existing beyond the norm.

A living buoy within the sea
fighting to stay alive,
like so much organic debris,
waiting for opportunity to arrive.

Drifting along currents of ocean,
these non-motile species
lack locomotion.

Sharing elemental riches
in return for defense….

Oh, little Radiolaria -
so no-nonsense.

Clandestine Chimaera

In a lightless kingdom
the deepest dwellers lie,
armorless and staring
with pale, reflective eyes.

Stitched and sown together,
adrift in the lonely blue
lives a mysterious, ghostly beauty
always shying out of view.

A Timeless Worm

Living on land, and sea, and inside
the bodies of many -
there's no place to hide.

We should seek to know
this champion of time
and not run in fear
of its regenerative slime.

They survive in a world
which misunderstands
the prehistoric truth
a flatworm commands.

Capable of renewing
itself inside and out
is a skill worth pursuing
and learning about.

The very first of so many kinds
a flatworm knows no bounds
An innovation of natural design,
a body driven by that which confounds.

Within skin that breathes

lives that head that leads
undeterred by damage and disease;
thus resilient invertebrates may do as they
please.

The Littlest Bat

Near the river in a limestone cave
the small creatures discovered
in Myanmar's southern lands
slumber and dream of beetle feasts.

At birth barely bigger
than the size of a pea,
these miraculous mammals
are miniature beasts.

The bumblebee bat
who can sit on one finger
was found by Kitti Thonglongya
with it's little hog nose.

Unknown to the world
before the year 1974,
now this tiny critter
faces many woes.

Without our flying mammal friends
the forests would die.
The insects uneaten
would blacken the sky.

Now the littlest bat
who could fit in your hand
must fight to survive
in their own homeland.

With their forests ablaze,
and monks causing distress
we must protect these small heroes,
for there's not many left.

The best natural pest control
devouring thousands each hour
and their fruit-eating cousins
pollinating each flower

without which we'd lose
bananas, mangoes, and dates
and avocados and peaches
would never appear on our plates.

Saving billions in just
crop damage each year,
these sweet sky puppies
are so very dear.

The Flying Lemur Facts

I stare in surprise when you call my name
It doesn't fit, says I.
And who could really lay out the blame
on a flying lemur that doesn't fly?

I'm not a lemur, either
but a tiny primate with wings.
And though I'll never soar
they aren't completely useless things.

I can glide from tree to tree
to delight in sap and fruit,
and though I'm webbed and winged
you might find me rather cute.

I'm the feather-light Colugo
bearing a baby in the flying membrane.
I seek a safe and quiet crevice
in my forested domain.

Language of Mycelium

Threading through an underground galaxy
I expand the hidden organic connections.

My network breathes and pulses
under the strata of perceptions.

I am alive and growing,
touching everything I can.

Always listening and feeling
so that I may understand

the secrets of the trees
and the songs of life
and death, and birth.

Endlessly reaching
to become one with the Earth.

Sparklemuffin

He rolls down under with his brothers
in a microworld,
jumping and shaking
for the eight-legged girls.

Painted by the rainbow
of a peacock trinity
this leg-waving arachnid's
a tiny dancing divinity.

A flashy jumping bean,
he relies upon height
of forty times his length -
an incredible sight.

No, he doesn't weave
silken webs in the night
for his weapon of choice
is the apex of sight.

The full visible spectrum
is the Sparklemufflin's tool
both inside and out,
a living, leaping jewel.

Luck of the Gerenuk

I cruise carefully on nimble limbs
long-necked lingering in the African Horn.
Dashing and darting from danger
through sand and prickled thorn.

Sometimes surviving without a single sip
of the sparkling waters that elsewhere abound,
but instead forever reaching
for what little this desert has around.

I grew long and well-adapted
to see and hear through the muck,
but sometimes all survival
is simply stupid luck!

Skink's Sapphire Secret

Atop a cushion of rock
I lounge and wait among
borrowed shadowy burrows
flashing my azure tongue.

With bugs and berries on the menu
living's not so grim.
I can feast without much effort,
no need for staying slim.

I am of low maintenance
and rather tame, it's true.
But at any given moment
I can flash my wild blue

distasteful-looking lingua
at an enemy, or two.

Night of the Werewolf Mouse

Beneath a twinkling sky
of sharp eyes and searching claws
a skittering soul scurries
on tiny, intent paws.

Hunting by moonlight
she spies the scorpion's shape.
A tail silhouetted by death
offers no gentle escape.

But she is undaunted by his sting
and prepares for a fight.
Ears twitch and eyes lock,
they circle in the night.

The battle comes to blows
and the tail strikes her hide,
but she has a superpower
keeping fate on her side.

A carnivorous mouse
so fierce you can believe
that she will survive
with this trick up her sleeve -

she is immune to his venom
and can strike like a cat
preying on arachnids like scorpions
and laying them out flat.

Once she has dined
she continues her nightly prowls,
and when the moon is full
throws her head back
and howls.

Home of the Pink Fairy Armadillo

She lies in wait
in the Argentina dunes
plated in pretty pink keratin
and peppered with fine, creamy hair.
Her name means "little armored one",
but she seeks the simple solace
of dining on snails in warm sand.
Small and sweet, yet wild at heart,
she wilts away when kept behind bars.
This tiny creature makes her home in the Earth,
thriving best under her native stars.

Jumping Jerboa

Leaping through life,
never time to slow.
Never at eye level,
erratically on the go.

Must be quick and nimble,
flying over dirt.
Can't stop for even a sip -
always on alert.

Looking all around
using sight, and sound , and smell.
Can she ever slow down?
Only time will tell.

Africa's Hidden Monkey

Shrouded by Congo jungle
is an unusual Lomami being,
and only tribesmen can hear
where their hauntingly beautiful cries ring.

Resonating through the forest,
they then watch with human eyes
for the prowling, howling hunters
veiled by natural disguise.

Deemed wise and insightful
with a silent and stunning repose,
a haunting portrait of intelligence
the Lesula's face bestows.

They are the Big-Headed Turtle

When your home is a part of you,
you must live within your own depth.
Swim in softer water,
and watch where you step.

Living in a body that doesn't fit
changes the way you move.
You will learn how to climb
in a world that disapproves.

Conquer impossible heights,
scaling soaring columns above.
You seek out other shelters
for safety, life, and love.

Careful not to disappear
into memory and bone,
you must carry thoughtfully
the part of you that's home.